Foreword

JN025079

　著者の Richard Carpenter 氏（有名な Carpenters の Karen の兄と同姓同名で 2 歳違い）は、ニューヨークのブルックリンで誕生し、1968 年に来日して米軍の横須賀基地に勤務、1970 年に除隊後は日本で暮らすことを決意し、日本語を学ぶとともに英語講師として教鞭を執るようなりますが、1976 年に転職してアメリカの出版社で営業の職に就きます。1986 年から 1990 年まではシアトルで暮らしていましたが、1990 年に再来日して東京・神田の雄松堂に勤務し、15 年間海外の版元との間を繋ぐ任を負いながら、企画・出版にも携わり、定年退職後から 2018 年までは、プレゼンの仕方、会議や打ち合わせへの対応といったビジネス英語の講師として勤務し、ユニクロなどの企業へ派遣され、早朝から都内を飛び回る日々を送っていました。現在は自宅で Skype を使った英会話レッスンをおこなっています。

　本書には氏が執筆されたショートエッセイが 15 編収録されています。テーマもアメリカのショッピング・モール、登山、旅、（コンピュータの）バグ、書物、博物館、英単語、スタバ、パディントン、ジェンダー、エンパイア・ステート・ビル、ウイルス、ハロウィン、イディオム、ウィンザー城など実に多種多様です。本文の平均語数は 210 語ながら、読者に飽きさせず読ませる書き手として定評のある人で、松柏社刊行の *Focus on Reading!* はロングセラーになっています。皆さんにもきっと楽しく読んでいただけると思います。

　私がこのテキストで皆さんに学習していただきたいと思うことが 2 つあります。1 つは語彙数を増やすこと、もう 1 つは文法力を身につけることです。語彙力を増強していただくために Vocabulary Check Before Reading と Synonyms Check Before Reading の 2 種類の単語問題を作成しました。この 2 つの単語問題に出てくる単語はしっかりマスターしてください。読解力を伸ばすためには、語彙数を増やすことが必要不可欠です。文法は文を正確に読むために非常に重要です。文法の解説はかなり詳しくおこないましたので、理解できるまで何回も読み直していただければと思います。

　2019 年秋

森永弘司

Contents

Mall of America (MOA)

Grammar Tip Before Reading

▶ 過去分詞の副詞用法

　この Unit の英文の冒頭にある Located は過去形、それとも過去分詞？

　正解は過去分詞です。過去形が主語なしで使われることはありません。また過去形ならば and という接続詞がないと、MOA is ... attraction. という文につなげることはできません。

　過去分詞には４つの使い方

　❶完了　❷受け身　❸過去分詞形容詞用法　❹分詞構文

　がありますが、この Located はどの用法で使われているでしょうか？

　正解は❹の分詞構文です。分詞構文は過去分詞の副詞用法で、接続詞の働きも兼ねています。副詞の基本的な働きは動詞の修飾（説明）です。この文では MOA is ... attraction. という主節の文の is を修飾する働きをしています。補う接続詞はこの場合は理由を表す because か as が適切でしょう。つまり、Located で始まるこの文は下の意味になるというわけです。

Located only 1.5 miles (2.4km) by Light Rail from St. Paul/Minneapolis International Airport, MOA <u>is</u> a huge tourist attraction.

　MOA はセント・ポール国際空港から軽量軌道交通を利用するとわずか 1.5 マイル（2.4 キロ）の距離なので、観光客にとってとても魅力ある場所である。

Vocabulary Check Before Reading

本文に出てくる単語の意味として正しいものを選択肢の中から選びなさい。

1. billion　　**2.** revenue　　**3.** theme　　**4.** aquarium　　**5.** destination

ⓐ テーマ　　ⓑ 水族館　　ⓒ 10 億　　ⓓ 目的地　　ⓔ 収入

Audio 02

Reading Passage

Located only 1.5 miles (2.4km) by Light Rail from St. Paul/ Minneapolis International Airport, MOA is a huge tourist attraction. With 555 stores and 50 restaurants, there are many things to do in the Mall. MOA built in 1992 occupies 500,000 m^2 of floor space. MOA receives about 42,000,000 visitors per year and generates over 2 billion dollars of revenue for Minnesota. 5

For attractions there are Nickelodeon Universe® the nation's largest indoor theme park, Sea Life® Minnesota Aquarium, Flyover America and many others. MOA holds many events throughout the year such as Music in the Mall, Regional Yo-yo Championship and 10 LiveWell Expo to name a few.

Restaurants include names such as Bubba Gump Shrimp Co., Cadillac Ranch, Chipotle, Great American Cookies and Popeyes Louisiana 15 Kitchen. There are quite a few Japanese restaurants as well.

So if your destination is MOA you can stay at one of the many hotels in the Minneapolis area all of which are 20 conveniently located to MOA.

Some interesting facts about MOA are:
1. The total area of MOA is as large as 9 Yankee Stadiums.
2. 70°F degrees is the inside temperature regardless of what season it is. This temperature is maintained by skylights, passive residual 25 heat from lights and humans.
3. Recycles more than 60% of its 32,000 tons of waste per year.
4. MOA has 30,000 live plants and 400 live trees.

NOTES

Light Rail 軽量軌道交通（ここではメトロ交通局の運営するライトレール Hiawatha Line のこと）
®=registered 登録商標
Flyover America 最先端の特殊効果を駆使した疑似飛行体験を経験できる施設
to name a few 2、3 例を挙げると
Bubba Gump Shrimp アカデミー作品賞を受賞した『フォレスト・ガンプ』をテーマにして作られたアメリカのシーフード・レストラン
70°F degrees 摂氏を表す C や華氏を表す F の表記が使われていない場合もあるが、70 度という室内の温度は日本の摂氏ではあり得ないので、F の表記がなくても「華氏 70 度」を意味する。摂氏の換算式は、(5 ÷ 9)×(華氏－32)、華氏の換算式は、(9 ÷ 5)×摂氏＋32。
regardless of ~ ～にかかわらず
skylight 天窓

(=) Synonyms Check After Reading

本文に出てきた動詞・語句の意味として近いものを選択肢の中から選びなさい。

1. occupy	ⓐ ball park
2. generate	ⓑ during
3. throughout	ⓒ too
4. include	ⓓ contain
5. name	ⓔ take
6. as well	ⓕ keep
7. temperature	ⓖ heat
8. stadium	ⓗ garbage
9. maintain	ⓘ mention
10. waste	ⓙ produce

○× True or False

本文の内容を正しく示している英文には T、誤っている英文には F を記入しなさい。

_____ **1.** Moa is located in the state of Wisconsin.

_____ **2.** It is a huge tourist attraction and receives over 40,000,000 visitors per year.

_____ **3.** There are many plants and trees around the outside of the mall.

 **Comprehension** Check

質問の答えとして正しいものを 3 つの選択肢の中から選びなさい。

1. How much money does MOA generate for Minnesota?

 a. over 20,000,000,000 dollars
 b. over 2,000,000,000 dollars
 c. over 200,000,000,000 dollars

2. How many restaurants are there in MOA?

 a. There are very few restaurants.
 b. There are several restaurants.
 c. There are a lot of restaurants.

3. How many degrees is the inside of MOA?

 a. 21°C.　**b.** 70°C.　　**c.** 17°F.

 Audio 03

 Listening for Information

音声を聞いて、答えとして正しいものを選択肢の中から選びましょう。本文に出てくる数字などのデータを正しく把握できているか確認しましょう。

1. a. 500,000　　**b.** 150,000　　　**c.** 50,000

2. a. as big as 3 Yankee Stadiums
 b. as big as 6 Yankee Stadiums
 c. as big as 9 Yankee Stadiums

3. a. 30,400　　**b.** 30,000　　　**c.** 400

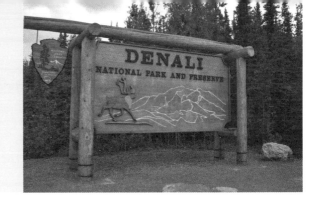

Denali

Grammar Tip Before Reading

▶ 不定詞の名詞＆形容詞用法

これから読む英文では不定詞が使われています。英語の名詞の文中での基本的な働きは、❶主語　❷動詞の目的語　❸前置詞の目的語　❹補語の４つです。不定詞は❸前置詞の目的語にはなれないので注意しましょう。

ここで使われる不定詞名詞用法は下記のように❷動詞の目的語として使われています。

continue　to climb
<u>　↑　</u>　　　　<u>　　　　</u>
　動詞　　　　　目的語（英語では目的語になれる品詞は名詞のみ）

英語の形容詞の文中での基本的な働きは、名詞修飾と補語の２つです。
この Unit で使っている不定詞形容詞用法はすべて名詞修飾の働きをしています。

the best season　to visit

the first climber　to reach　the peak

the first Japanese　to climb　Denali

the first person　to do　it

不定詞の形は「to＋動詞の原形」で見つけやすいのですが、用法に名詞、形容詞、副詞と３つあり、英文を正確に読む際にこの用法の識別が重要になるのでしっかりマスターしましょう。

Vocabulary Check Before Reading

本文に出てくる単語の意味として正しいものを選択肢の中から選びなさい。

1. climber　　**2.** mission　　**3.** summit　　**4.** descent　　**5.** crevasse

ⓐ 下山　　ⓑ 裂け目　　ⓒ 登山家　　ⓓ 頂上　　ⓔ 任務

Reading Passage

1　The highest peak in Alaska and all of North America (6190m) and the third highest above sea level in the Seven Summits, Denali was originally named Mt. McKinley. However the indigenous people Koyukon who have lived in the area have called it "Denali" for centuries. ₅

2　Denali is also a National Park and many visitors go there in

summer which is the best season to visit. It is such a high mountain that it has its own weather system and one must be prepared for sudden changes ₁₀ in the weather.

3　The first climbers to reach the peak were four men in 1910 but this was viewed in doubt. After that in 1913 two men Hudson Stuck and Harry ₁₅ Karskens successfully reached the top.

4　Many climbers today continue to climb the mountain using the West Buttress Route, considered the safest route. Climbers usually climb in summer and a typical climb takes two to four weeks.

5　Naomi Uemura a Japanese solo adventurer was the first Japanese ₂₀ to climb Denali and he did this in summer 1970 becoming the first person to do it alone. However he wanted to do a solo winter climb, an extremely dangerous mission. He did reach the summit but on the descent he was lost and never found again. It is believed that he may have fallen into a large crevasse and died there. Unfortunately his ₂₅ body was never found.

NOTES

indigenous　現地の、その土地の
It is such a high mountain that ~　それ（デナリ）はとても高い山なので~です
Naomi Uemura a Japanese solo adventurer　Naomi Uemura と a Japanese solo adventurer は同格の関係にある。同格は名詞を別の名詞で言い換えたもの。この文の主語である Naomi Uemura を a Japanese solo adventurer という別の名詞で言い換えている。意味は「日本人の単独冒険家であるウエムラナオミ（植村直己）」。
It is believed that ~　It は仮主語で、真主語は that 以下の文である。「that 以下であると信じられている」。
his body　彼の死体

(=) Synonyms Check After Reading

本文に出てきた動詞・語句の意味として近いものを選択肢の中から選びなさい。

1. name
2. prepare
3. reach
4. view
5. in doubt
6. continue
7. take
8. be lost
9. believe
10. fall

ⓐ arrive
ⓑ uncertain
ⓒ arrange
ⓓ drop
ⓔ keep
ⓕ call
ⓖ stray
ⓗ regard
ⓘ think
ⓙ need

○× True or False

本文の内容を正しく示している英文には T、誤っている英文には F を記入しなさい。

_____ 1. Denali is the third highest peak in the world.

_____ 2. Many climbers climb in spring.

_____ 3. Naomi Uemura may have fallen into a crevasse and died.

Comprehension Check

質問の答えとして正しいものを 3 つの選択肢の中から選びなさい。

1. How long have people Koyukon called Mt. Mckinley Denali?

   a. For thousands of years
   b. For ten thousands of years
   c. For hundreds of years

2. Who were the first climbers to reach the summit of Denali?

   a. Naomi Uemura
   b. Hudson Stuck and Harry Karskens
   c. Four men in 1910

3. When did Naomi Uemura die?

   a. When in a solo winter climb
   b. When in a solo summer climb
   c. When in a solo fall climb

🔊 Audio 05

 ## Listening for Information

音声を聞いて、答えとして正しいものを選択肢の中から選びましょう。本文に出てくる数字などのデータを正しく把握できているか確認しましょう。

1. a. Highest mountain in America
   b. Highest mountain in the world
   c. Highest mountain in South America

2. a. two to four weeks   **b.** two to four days
   c. two to four months

3. a. on the peak   **b.** on the descent   **c.** in a large crevasse

Get Your Kicks on Route 66

Grammar Tip Before Reading

▶過去分詞形容詞用法と現在分詞形容詞用法

この Unit の英文中で使われている過去分詞を紹介します。

・This little phrase taken from a song
　　　　↑
　　　　　　　過去分詞形容詞用法

・a song sung by Nat King Cole
　↑
　　　　過去分詞形容詞用法

現在分詞にも形容詞用法があり、本文中で使われている形容詞用法には以下の二つがあります。

・countless Americans looking for adventure
　　　　↑
　　　　　　　　　現在分詞形容詞用法

・Americans back to the route looking for adventure
　↑
　　　　　　　　現在分詞形容詞用法

ところが以下の二つの例は現在分詞の形容詞用法ではなく動名詞なのです。

・ camping ground
・ trucking industry

camping と trucking がなぜ現在分詞形容詞用法ではなく（動）名詞なのかを Unit 4 で説明します。

Vocabulary Check Before Reading

本文に出てくる単語の意味として正しいものを選択肢の中から選びなさい。

1. phrase　　**2.** adventure　　**3.** existence　　**4.** optimism　　**5.** lane

ⓐ 冒険　　ⓑ 楽観主義　　ⓒ 存在　　ⓓ 言い回し　　ⓔ 小道

Reading Passage

1 This little phrase taken from a song sung by Nat King Cole was a catch phrase for countless Americans looking for adventure. Route 66 became the designated route between Chicago and Los Angeles. It was one of the nation's main east-west arteries.

2 Route 66 was immortalized in John Steinbeck's book *Grapes of* 5 *Wrath*. Approximately 210,000 Americans migrated west to escape the devastating effects of the Dust Bowl. Route 66 brought work

and jobs to many Americans and helped to populate the west. Stores, gas stations, motels, and camping 10 grounds popped up along the road as more and more Americans bought cars after WWII.

3 Then in 1966 Americans tuned into the popular TV series "Route 15 66" which brought them back to the route looking for adventure. However the trucking industry expanded and so the US government passed the Federal Aid Highway Act. This act underwrote the cost of the Freeway system that now criss-crosses the USA. And eventually Route 66 fell into disrepair as more 20 motorists bypassed the route for the freeways.

4 Sections of the route still remain in existence and they are a symbol of America that reminds us of the spirit of optimism that people had after the Great Depression and a global war. It is still possible to drive sections of the route and take a trip down memory lane. 25

NOTES

    Get your kicks on Route 66　邦題「ルート 66」（Nat King Cole の代表曲の 1 つ。意味は「国道 66 号線で楽しくやろう」。）　**Nat King Cole (1919-65)** は、アメリカのスイング・ジャズ時代の名ピアニストで歌手。歌手としての代表作には、上記の「ルート 66」、「スターダスト」、「モナ・リザ」などがある。**the designated route**　指定された道路　**artery**　幹線道路　**John Steinbeck (1902-68)**　アメリカを代表する小説家・劇作家。1962 年にノーベル文学賞を受賞。代表作には『怒りの葡萄』、『エデンの東』、『二十日鼠と人間』などがある。　**Dust Bowl**　1930 年代に砂嵐の被害を受けた米国中南部の乾燥平原地帯　**pop up**　次々とできる　**tune into~**　～に敏感に反応する　**the Federal Aid Highway Act**　連邦補助高速道路法（1956 年に制定された、全長約 6 万 5,000 キロメートルの州間高速道路網を建設することを目的とする法律）　**criss-cross~**　～を縦横に走る　**fall into dispair**　荒廃する　**bypass**　～を迂回する　**remain in existence**　存在する　**the Great Depression**　大恐慌（1929 年に米国で始まった経済不況）　**a global war**　世界的な戦争　**take a trip down memory lane**　昔の思い出に浸る

(=) Synonyms

本文に出てきた動詞・語句の意味として近いものを選択肢の中から選びなさい。

1. look for
2. designate
3. immortalize
4. migrate
5. escape
6. populate
7. tune
8. underwrite
9. remain
10. remind

ⓐ commemorate
ⓑ search
ⓒ inhabit
ⓓ adjust
ⓔ get away
ⓕ move
ⓖ bring to mind
ⓗ continue to exist
ⓘ sponsor
ⓙ nominate

○× True or False

本文の内容を正しく示している英文には T、誤っている英文には F を記入しなさい。

_____ **1.** Route 66 connected Chicago to San Francisco.

_____ **2.** The "Grapes of Wrath" was written by Ernest Hemingway.

_____ **3.** The USA freeway system is now the fastest way to drive to your destination.

Comprehension Check

質問の答えとして正しいものを 3 つの選択肢の中から選びなさい。

1. How many Americans migrated west to escape the devastating effects of the Dust Bowl?

   a. About 21,000   **b.** About 2100,000   **c.** About 210,000

2. Why did the US government pass The Federal Aid Highway Act?

   a. Because more and more Americans bought cars
   b. Because TV series "Route 66" became popular
   c. Because the trucking industry expanded

3. What kind of spirit did American people have after The Great Depression and a global war?

   a. Adventure   **b.** Pessimism   **c.** Optimism

Audio 07

 ## Listening for Information

音声を聞いて、答えとして正しいものを選択肢の中から選びましょう。本文に出てくる数字などのデータを正しく把握できているか確認しましょう。

1. a. John Steinbeck
   b. Nat King Cole
   c. Grapes of Wrath

2. a. Because many motorists bypassed the route for the freeways
   b. Because more and more Americans bought cars
   c. Because countless Americans looked for adventure

3. a. The freeway system
   b. Route 66
   c. The spirit of optimism

Stop Bugging Me!

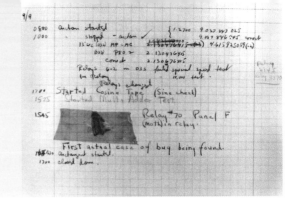

Grammar Tip Before Reading

　現在分詞の基本的な意味は「～しつつある」です。これを Unit 3 の camping と trucking に当てはめると、camping ground「キャンプしつつある土地」、trucking industry「トラック運送しつつある業界」という意味になりますが、2つとも意味がおかしいですね。

　現在分詞形容詞用法でも動名詞でも解釈できる文でその違いがわかります。
a dancing girl は「踊っている女の子」とも「踊り子」とも解釈できます。
　dancing が現在分詞形容詞用法の場合＝踊っている女の子
　dancing が動名詞の場合＝踊り子（＝ a girl for dancing「踊るための女の子」）

　つまり、下記のように解釈できるわけです。
　camping ground ＝キャンプするための土地＝キャンプ場
　trucking industry ＝トラック運送のための業界＝トラック運送業界

　動名詞の文中の働きは名詞と同じで、❶主語❷動詞の目的語❸前置詞の目的語❹補語の4つのいずれかで働きます。この Unit では2つの動名詞が使われていますが、その2つの動名詞とその働きがわかりますか？
　<u>Stop</u> Bugging Me!　Bugging は動詞 Stop の目的語
　<u>in</u> the switch thus hindering　hindering は前置詞 in の目的語

Vocabulary Check Before Reading

本文に出てくる単語の意味として正しいものを選択肢の中から選びなさい。

1. malfunction　　**2.** investigation　　**3.** moth　　**4.** operation　　**5.** rug

ⓐ 調査　　ⓑ （昆虫）ガ　　ⓒ 操作　　ⓓ 故障　　ⓔ 敷物

Reading Passage

1 What do you think the title means? Think of a mosquito which comes back many times to bite you and you shoo it away again and again. It *bothers* you so "bug" = "bother."

2 In 1878 Thomas Edison, an electrical engineer, used the word 5 "bugs" in a letter to describe little faults and difficulties and it then was used to describe mechanical malfunctions.

3 An American pioneer in the 10 development of computer software known as COBOL was Grace Hopper. During a test of the Mark II computer, the operators found that a relay switch was not working and upon investigation they had found that a moth was caught in the switch thus hindering its 15 operation. So they had to "debug" the switch. "Bug" then became known as a "glitch" or a small computer malfunction.

4 So "bug" has come into English and it is widely used to describe glitches in computers or computer software.

5 What is the difference between "bug" and "defect?" Basically a bug 20 is a fault in a program found during testing. A defect however is when the application does not conform to a required specification.

6 There are many other expressions using the word "bug." Can you figure out the following expressions?....."Millennium bug, Love bug, June bug, Bug off, Bug out." And how about this one......"as snug as a 25 bug in a rug?"

NOTES

Thomas Edison (1847-1931)　生涯の特許がアメリカで 1093 件、他国で 1300 件を超えるアメリカの実業家、発明王
COBOL　コンピューターのプログラミング言語の１つで、事務用のデータ処理に使用されている
Grace Hopper (1906-1992)　アメリカ海軍の軍人かつ計算機科学者で、COBOL の開発者である
Mark II　アメリカ初の電気機械式計算機である Mark I の後継機
glitch　コンピューターのトラブル、問題点
Millennium bug　コンピューターの 2000 年問題（2000 年になるとコンピューターが誤作動する可能性があるとされた問題）
love bug　ラブバグ（昆虫）米国南東部で春に発生し、自動車交通の障害になる虫
June bug　コフキコガネ（昆虫）
bug off　すばやく去る
bug out　急いで逃げ出す
as snug as a bug in a rug　ぬくぬくとして心地いい

本文に出てきた動詞・語句の意味として近いものを選択肢の中から選びなさい。

1. mean		ⓐ	make something/someone go away
2. bite		ⓑ	signify
3. shoo		ⓒ	disturb
4. bother		ⓓ	explain
5. describe		ⓔ	need
6. hinder		ⓕ	remove
7. debug		ⓖ	sting
8. conform		ⓗ	obey
9. require		ⓘ	annoy
10. figure out		ⓙ	understand

○× True or False

本文の内容を正しく示している英文には T、誤っている英文には F を記入しなさい。

_____ **1.** Thomas Edison was a computer engineer who used the word "bugs."

_____ **2.** A cockroach was found in the Mark II computer.

_____ **3.** "Bug" and "defect are similes.

💡 **Comprehension** Check

質問の答えとして正しいものを 3 つの選択肢の中から選びなさい。

1. What did Thomas Edison mean by the word "bugs"?

   a. Moths in the switch
   b. Little faults and difficulties
   c. Mechanical malfunctions

2. What is COBOL?

   a. The name of computer software
   b. The name of a moth
   c. The name of a small computer malfunction

3. What does millennium mean?

   a. For a hundred years
   b. For a thousand years
   c. For fifty years

. ⑴ **Audio 09**

Listening for Information

音声を聞いて、答えとして正しいものを選択肢の中から選びましょう。本文に出てくる数字などのデータを正しく把握できているか確認しましょう。

1. a. Thomas Edison   **b.** Grace Hopper   **c.** The operators

2. a. Thomas Edison   **b.** Grace Hopper   **c.** The operators

3. a. During investigation   **b.** During operation   **c.** During testing

Grammar Tip Before Reading

▶ 関係代名詞が普通の文を説明文に変える

　この Unit の英文では 4 つ関係代名詞が使われています。関係代名詞は英文では頻繁に使用されます。

　He showed me the fish. という文と He had caught the fish in the river. という文を関係代名詞を使って 1 つの文にすると、

　He showed me the fish which he had caught in the river.

　彼は川で捕まえた魚を私に見せてくれた。

となります。この時、関係代名詞の which はどのような働きをしているのでしょうか？

上記の訳を見ると、which はまったく訳出されていませんね。ということは which は意味的な働きはしていないということになります。実は which は 普通の文 を 説明文 に変える働きをしているのです。

　He had caught the fish in the river. の the fish を代名詞の it に置き換える➡ He had caught it in the river. ➡次に it を which に変える➡ He had caught which in the river. ➡最後に which を文の初めに持ってきます。すると which he had caught in the river. という文ができ➡ 説明文 が完成します。なぜ which という関係代名詞を文頭に移動させるのでしょうか？　実は関係代名詞は、 説明文 の開始を知らせる働きもしているからです。しっかり覚えておきましょう。

Vocabulary Check Before Reading

本文に出てくる単語の意味として正しいものを選択肢の中から選びなさい。

1. countryside　　**2.** fossil　　**3.** evidence　　**4.** landscape　　**5.** castle

ⓐ 田舎　　ⓑ 化石　　ⓒ 城　　ⓓ 景色、風景　　ⓔ 証拠

Reading Passage

1 Located in the southwest of England, Cotswolds is an area of natural beauty. Containing beautiful countryside and rolling hills, attractive villages were built from the Cotswold stone. This limestone is rich in fossils and is golden colored. This stone has been used to build the row houses which contribute to the unique features of the ₅ whole area. It is almost like a fairy tale.

2 The Cotswolds has a long history. There is evidence of Neolithic settlements and remains of the Bronze and Iron Age forts. Later the Romans built villas and paths there. During the Middle Ages the area became famous for sheep and the wool trade which brought in much ₁₀ money. Churches were then built using the stone.

3 There are many villages which typify British culture along with the natural landscape. The Cotswolds receives about 23 million visitors per year.

4 The picturesque towns and villages, which are built of the ₁₅ limestone, have appeared in many movies, the most recent in some scenes of the "Harry Potter" movies. There are row houses or individual homes with tailored British gardens, churches, castles and manor houses to name a few.

5 You can enjoy Bribery a typical Cotswolds village or the row houses ₂₀ in Broadway, Worcestershire and Sudeley Castle built in the 15th century with its "secret garden."

6 Cotswolds can be accessed by expressway or high speed rail.

NOTES

rolling hills　ゆるやかに起伏する丘　**Cotswold stone**　イギリスのコッツウォルズ地方で産出される天然の石灰石　**limestone**　石灰石　**fairy tale**　妖精物語、おとぎ話　**Neolithic**　新石器時代　**settlement**　社会　**Bronze and Iron Age**　青銅器時代と鉄器時代　**fort**　城砦（とりで）　**the Middle Ages**　中世（西洋では西ローマ帝国が滅亡した 476 年から 15 世紀のルネッサンスまでを指す）　**along with ~**　～に加えて　**Harry Potter**　Ｊ・Ｋ・ローリングによって書かれた世界的ベストセラーとなった児童文学、ファンタジー小説　**tailored**　手入れの行き届いた　**secret garden**　スードリー城には８つのガーデンがあり、その中に「秘密の庭園」と呼ばれる庭がある

本文に出てきた動詞・語句の意味として近いものを選択肢の中から選びなさい。

1.	contribute	ⓐ	give
2.	become	ⓑ	represent
3.	bring	ⓒ	be given
4.	typify	ⓓ	come to be
5.	receive	ⓔ	take
6.	appear	ⓕ	become visible
7.	tailor	ⓖ	call
8.	name	ⓗ	take delight
9.	enjoy	ⓘ	approach
10.	access	ⓙ	customize

○× **True or False**

本文の内容を正しく示している英文には T、誤っている英文には F を記入しなさい。

_____ **1.** The limestone is indigenous to the Cotswolds area.

_____ **2.** The Cotswolds stone was used to build walls only around homes.

_____ **3.** Many visitors go to the Cotswolds area every year.

Comprehension Check

質問の答えとして正しいものを 3 つの選択肢の中から選びなさい。

1. What is the unique feature of Cotswolds?

    a. Natural beauty
    b. Beautiful countryside
    c. Row houses

2. What is the evidence of a very long history of Cotswolds?

    a. Old churches
    b. Villas and paths
    c. Remains of the Bronze and Iron Age forts.

3. How can we access Cotswolds?

    a. By bicycle   **b.** By train   **c.** On foot

Audio 11

Listening for Information

音声を聞いて、答えとして正しいものを選択肢の中から選びましょう。本文に出てくる数字などのデータを正しく把握できているか確認しましょう。

1. a. Building the Bronze and Iron Age forts
    b. Building villas and paths
    c. Building row houses

2. a. Sheep and the wool trade
    b. The picturesque towns and villages
    c. Neolithic settlements

3. a. About 230,000,000
    b. About 23,000,000
    c. About 2,300,000

OMG
What Is
THAT?

Grammar Tip Before Reading

▶ 関係代名詞は形容詞の働きをする

　関係代名詞が作る節（文）は形容詞の働きをして先行詞と呼ばれる名詞を修飾しています。関係代名詞は関係代名詞が作る節（形容詞節）の中で❶主語❷動詞の目的語❸前置詞の目的語❹補語のいずれかの働きをしています。

① Something ②<u>which</u> is rather gross is ③ the nine-foot-long human colon ④ <u>that</u> contained over 40 pounds of fecal matter removed from the remains of a man.

ここには関係代名詞が２つ含まれています。②が形容詞節で、関係代名詞の which は節の中で主語の働きをしています。そして②の形容詞節が①の名詞を修飾（説明）し、④が形容詞節で、関係代名詞の that は節の中で主語の働きをし、④の形容詞節が③の名詞を修飾（説明）しています。

And finally there is the body of the "Soap Lady," ①<u>whose</u> corpse turned itself into a soapy substance called "adipocere" better known as grave wax.

①が形容詞節で、関係代名詞 whose（正確には関係形容詞）は節の中で形容詞の働きをしています。

　先程の説明と違うなと思われたのではないでしょうか？　whose の働きをさらに簡単な例文で説明します。

I have a friend whose father is a musician.

この文では、whose father is a musician が形容詞節で、a friend という名詞を修飾しています。しかし、主語は father です。この文は、I have a friend という文と His father is a musician という文を whose を使って書き換えたものなので、whose は代名詞の所有格 his と同じ働きをしています。所有格の働きは名詞修飾なので、whose の文中の働きは形容詞です。従って whose は実は関係形容詞と呼ぶべきものなのです。

Vocabulary Check Before Reading

本文に出てくる単語の意味として正しいものを選択肢の中から選びなさい。

1. oddity　　**2.** specimen　　**3.** display　　**4.** corpse　　**5.** wax

ⓐ ろう　　ⓑ 死体　　ⓒ 展示　　ⓓ 標本　　ⓔ 奇態

🔊 **Audio 12**

Reading Passage

1 "Wacky, gross, horrific!" are some of the adjectives that are used. Others however are "educational, resourceful and an eye opener."

2 Welcome to the Mütter Museum located in Philadelphia, USA. This museum contains a collection of medical oddities, anatomical and pathological specimens, wax models, and antique medical equipment. 5 The collection was donated by Dr. Thomas Dent Mütter in 1858 and was for biomedical research and education.

3 The Mütter Museum is best known for the Hyrtl Skull Collection and other anatomical specimens. It includes a wax model of a woman with a horn growing out of her forehead and several wax molds of 10

untreated conditions of the head. It also has the tallest skeleton currently on display in North America. Something which is rather gross is the nine-foot-long 15 human colon that contained over 40 pounds of fecal matter removed from the remains of a man. This man appeared in a sideshow act called the "Human Balloon." And finally there is the body of the 20 "Soap Lady," whose corpse turned itself into a soapy substance called "adipocere" better known as grave wax. Many wax models from the early 19th century are on display as are numerous preserved organs and body parts.

4 The Mütter Museum helps the public to appreciate the mysteries 25 and beauty of the human body and to understand the history of diagnosis and treatment of disease.

NOTES

wacky　風変わりな	gross　気味の悪い
horrific　恐ろしい、ぞっとする	resourceful　資源に富んだ
eye opener　とても啓発的なもの	anatomical　解剖の
pathological　病理組織の	equipment　器具
biomedical　生物医学の	forehead　額（発音に注意）
skeleton　骸骨	foot　フィート（長さの単位）１フィートは、30.48 センチ
colon　結腸	pound　ポンド（重さの単位）１ポンドは、約 454 グラム
fecal matter　大便	remains　遺体
sideshow act　余興	balloon　風船
corpse　（人間の）死体	substance　物質
adipocere　屍蝋（ロウのように変化した死体）	grave wax　屍蝋
... <u>as</u> are ...　関係代名詞の as。形容詞節の中で主語として働いている。	
organ　臓器	diagnosis　診断

(=) Synonyms

本文に出てきた動詞・語句の意味として近いものを選択肢の中から選びなさい。

1. use		ⓐ cover	
2. contain		ⓑ comprehend	
3. donate		ⓒ take away	
4. include		ⓓ stretch	
5. grow		ⓔ offer	
6. remove		ⓕ take in	
7. turn		ⓖ keep	
8. preserve		ⓗ change	
9. appreciate		ⓘ utilize	
10. understand		ⓙ recognize	

○✕ True or False

本文の内容を正しく示している英文には T、誤っている英文には F を記入しなさい。

_____ **1.** The Mutter Museum is located in Chicago, Illinois.

_____ **2.** The museum contains specimens of animals from North America.

_____ **3.** The purpose of the museum is to show the beauty of the human body.

Comprehension Check

質問の答えとして正しいものを 3 つの選択肢の中から選びなさい。

1. What is the best description of the collection of the Mutter Museum?

    a. It is not wacky but educational
    b. It is both wacky and educational
    c. It is neither wacky nor educational.

2. What was the relation between Dr. Mutter and the Mutter Museum?

    a. He was the founder of the Museum.
    b. He was the donator of the Museum
    c. He was the donator of the collection of the Museum

3. What is something rather gross in the collection?

    a. The nine-foot-long human colon
    b. A wax model of a woman with a horn
    c. The body of the "Soapy Lady"

. 》》 Audio 13

Listening for Information

音声を聞いて、答えとして正しいものを選択肢の中から選びましょう。本文に出てくる数字などのデータを正しく把握できているか確認しましょう。

1. a. Wax models   **b.** Fossils   **c.** Fine arts

2. a. About 284 centimeters
    b. About 264 centimeters
    c. About 274 centimeters

3. a. About 18.2 kilograms
    b. About 19.2 kilograms
    c. About 20.2 kilograms

Scrabble

Grammar Tip Before Reading

▶ 関係代名詞と関係副詞の違い

Unit 6 の英文から、ある関係代名詞が含まれている文を引用します。

Many wax models from the early 19th century are on display as are numerous preserved organs and body parts

たくさんの保存された臓器や体の色々な部位と同じくらい多くの 19 世紀に作られたロウ人形が展示されている。

上記では as が関係代名詞として使われています。もしも as が接続詞の as であれば、必ず as 以下に完全な文が来ますが、上の文では as 以下に主語がありません。

関係代名詞 as が主語として働く例は少ないですが、as には関係代名詞の用法もあるということを覚えておきましょう。

関係代名詞と同じように、文の形で形容詞の働きをして名詞を説明する品詞として副詞節があります。

Scoring is based on the board where the letters land, e.g., double or triple letter or double or triple word.

この where は関係副詞です。関係副詞は節の中で副詞として働きます。

「これは彼が生まれた家です」という文を、関係代名詞を使って書くと、

This is the house (in which he was born) or (which he was born in.) となり、これを関係副詞を使って書くとこうなります。

⇒ This is the house (where he was born.)

関係代名詞が（　　　）の形容詞節の中で前置詞の目的語で働いているのに対し、where は副詞で働いています。関係代名詞と関係副詞の違いをしっかりと理解しておきましょう。

Vocabulary Check Before Reading

本文に出てくる単語の意味として正しいものを選択肢の中から選びなさい。

1. outage　　**2.** hurricane　　**3.** variation　　**4.** president　　**5.** combination

> ⓐ 組み合わせ　　ⓑ 停電　　ⓒ 社長　　ⓓ 大暴風　　ⓔ 変化を加えたもの

Reading Passage

1. In 1954 due to a power outage during a hurricane named "Hazel" I learned how to play Scrabble by candlelight.

2. In 1938 Alfred Mosher Butts created a variation of an original game called "Lexiko" and re-named it "Criss-Crosswords." Then in 1948 James Brunot bought the rights to the game and changed and ⁵ simplified the rules and renamed it "Scrabble." He had a winner! The word "scrabble" means "to scratch frantically."After that the president of Macy's Department Store bought one million games and it became a popular board game.

3. The game is now sold globally and is available in 29 languages. ¹⁰

4. Easy to play, each player has seven letters and words are formed both vertically and horizontally. Word combinations can also be made. Scoring is based on the board ¹⁵ where the letters land, e.g., double or triple letter or double or triple word. By using all seven letters, you get a bonus of 50 points.

5. Scrabble can be played anywhere and it is a great way to learn ²⁰ English words. A lot of words are simply three or four letters. It is also a great way to have fun with your classmates and learn English words at the same time.

6. Let's play Scrabble to learn English words!

NOTES

candle　ロウソク
right　権利
re-name　新しい名前をつける
frantically　猛烈に
board game　盤上でする遊び
globally　世界中で
Easy to play　Easy の前に Being が省略された分詞構文。意味は「ゲームをする人は誰でも簡単にプレイできる」。
letter　文字
vertically　垂直に、縦に
horizontally　水平に、横に
scoring　得点
e. g.《ラテン語》= exempli gratia　例えば
great　素晴らしい、とてもいい

本文に出てきた動詞・語句の意味として近いものを選択肢の中から選びなさい。

1. learn
2. create
3. change
4. simplify
5. scratch
6. buy
7. sell
8. play
9. form
10. base

ⓐ produce
ⓑ be bought
ⓒ found
ⓓ amuse oneself
ⓔ facilitate
ⓕ shape
ⓖ alter
ⓗ rub
ⓘ study
ⓙ purchase

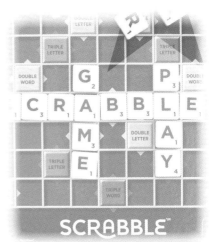

○× **True or False**

本文の内容を正しく示している英文には T、誤っている英文には F を記入しなさい。

_____ **1.** During a typhoon I learned how to play Scrabble.

_____ **2.** The president of Macy's Department Store bought a hundred thousand games.

_____ **3.** A lot of the words are three or four letter words.

💡 **Comprehension** Check

質問の答えとして正しいものを 3 つの選択肢の中から選びなさい。

1. What was the original game of Scrabble called?

    a. Hazel   **b.** Narcy   **c.** Lexiko

2. Who bought the rights to the game and named it "Scrabble"?

    a. James Brunot
    b. Alfred Mosher Butts
    c. The president of Macy's Department Store

3. What is Scrabble a great way to learn?

    a. English grammar
    b. English Pronunciation
    c. English Vocabulary

🔊 **Audio 15**

👂 **Listening** for Information

音声を聞いて、答えとして正しいものを選択肢の中から選びましょう。本文に出てくる数字などのデータを正しく把握できているか確認しましょう。

1. a. In 1954   **b.** In 1938   **c.** In 1948

2. a. 100,000   **b.** 10,000   **c.** 1,000,000

3. a. 29   **b.** 50   **c.** 100

Starbucks

Grammar ~~Tip Before Reading~~

▶ 原形不定詞を取る動詞

この Unit の英文中の and help make the world a little better の　部の make は原形不定詞 と呼ばれる to が付かない不定詞です。従ってここでは make は動詞 help の目的語である名詞用法として働いています。

原形不定詞を取る動詞には使役動詞（have, make, let）と知覚動詞（五感に関連した動詞、see, hear, feel, taste, smell, etc.）がありますが、help も原形不定詞を取る頻度がとても高い動詞です。

英語では特別なイディオムを除けば、原形を使用する5つの場所があります。使役動詞と知覚動詞を除く他の4つの場所とは、❶命令文❷助動詞の後❸不定詞の後❹仮定法現在です。ここでは❹仮定法現在に関して説明します。

The rule requires that all employees be present.
「規則では従業員全員が出席しなければならない。」

上記の be は be 動詞の原形ですね。要求や命令などを表す動詞（require, request, demand, order など）が名詞節を目的語として取る場合、目的節の中の動詞が原形を取ることが多いです。この時の原形が仮定法現在と呼ばれます。

英語の例外が絶対にない規則に、動詞の現在形と過去形は述語動詞（「普通動詞」と呼んでいる動詞）があります。be 動詞の原形は be で、現在形は is, am, are なので、be 動詞の場合は簡単に識別できますが、一般動詞の場合は、一部の不規則動詞を除けば、三単現の -s が付く場合以外は、原形と現在形の識別はできません。しかし原形を使用する5つの場所以外で使われていたら、その動詞は現在形であると確定できるわけです。

Vocabulary ~~Check Before Reading~~

本文に出てくる単語の意味として正しいものを選択肢の中から選びなさい。

1. partner　　**2.** location　　**3.** beans　　**4.** customer　　**5.** atmosphere

ⓐ 常連客　　ⓑ 雰囲気　　ⓒ 豆　　ⓓ 共同経営者　　ⓔ 所在地

Reading Passage

1 According to its website, Starbucks says "Every day, we go to work hoping to do two things: share great coffee with our friends and help make the world a little better. It was true when the first Starbucks opened in 1971, and it's just as true today."

2 Do you know where the first Starbucks store was opened? Founded ₅ by three partners, who were students at the University of San Francisco, it was a single store located in Pike Place Market, Seattle and it still retains this location to this day. At first Starbucks sold only roasted whole coffee beans and later coffee machines. Brewing the actual coffee came much later. After that, a variety of coffees, ₁₀ sandwiches and pastries were added. The name "Starbucks" was inspired by the novel "Moby Dick" which evoked the feeling of the seafaring tradition.

3 Gradually expanding its market, in 1996 it opened its Tokyo store with a bright relaxed and clean air atmosphere behind Matsuya ₁₅ Department Store. There are now over 1,000 stores throughout Japan. Starbucks has always kept its family style atmosphere so that customers can relax while enjoying a cup of coffee.

4 Nowadays you can see many people using their computers or chatting with friends or just killing time at any Starbucks in Tokyo. ₂₀

N O T E S

According to~　～によれば
Founded by three partners　分詞構文。意味は「3人の共同経営者によって設立された時には」。
Seattle　アメリカのワシントン州にある都市
whole coffee bean　（グラインダーで）ひいていないコーヒー豆
pastry　焼き菓子の総称
Moby Dick　『白鯨』（1851年にアメリカの作家ハーマン・メルヴィルによって書かれた小説。Starbucksという店名は、この小説に登場する一等航海士の名前であるStarbuckに由来するという説がある。）
Matsuya Department Store　1919年に設立された日本の老舗百貨店
kill time　時間をつぶす

(=) Synonyms

本文に出てきた動詞・語句の意味として近いものを選択肢の中から選びなさい。

1. hope
2. share
3. help
4. open
5. roast
6. brew
7. add
8. inspire
9. expand
10. relax

ⓐ produce
ⓑ make
ⓒ start a business
ⓓ parch
ⓔ assist
ⓕ increase
ⓖ divide
ⓗ wish
ⓘ relieve
ⓙ enlarge

○× True or False

本文の内容を正しく示している英文には T、誤っている英文には F を記入しなさい。

_____ **1.** Starbucks opened in 1971 in San Francisco.

_____ **2.** Moby Dick was a movie about spaceships.

_____ **3.** Starbuck's atmosphere is a family style and you can relax there while enjoying your coffee.

Comprehension Check

質問の答えとして正しいものを 3 つの選択肢の中から選びなさい。

1. How many people founded Starbucks?

    a. Two   **b.** Three   **c.** Four

2. Where was the first Starbucks store opened?

    a. In San Francisco
    b. In Tokyo
    c. In Seattle

3. What did Starbucks sell at first?

    a. Coffee machine
    b. A variety of coffee
    c. Roasted whole coffee

.))) **Audio 17**

 ## Listening for Information

音声を聞いて、答えとして正しいものを選択肢の中から選びましょう。本文に出てくる数字などのデータを正しく把握できているか確認しましょう。

1. a. In 1971   **b.** In 1980   **c.** In 1996

2. a. Behind Matsuya Department Store
    b. Near Tokyo station
    c. In Tokyo Disneyland

3. a. Over 100   **b.** Over 1,000   **c.** Over 10,000

A Famous Bear

Grammar Tip Before Reading

▶ この Unit までの復習

　最初に動詞＋名詞、形容詞、あるいは副詞の働きをする準動詞（動名詞、不定詞、現在分詞形容詞用法、現在分詞の分詞構文、過去分詞形容詞用法、過去分詞の分詞構文）を英文中から探し出してその働きを説明して下さい。

　次に形容詞節を探し出して文中での関係代名詞の働きを説明して下さい。それでは出てくる順番に説明していきます。冒頭は段落番号です。

1 不定詞 to write は動詞 inspired の補語なので、名詞用法か形容詞用法になる。

2 Sent to England~ の Sent は過去分詞の分詞構文なので、副詞用法になる。

3 wearing an old bush hat~ の wearing は現在分詞の分詞構文で、副詞用法になる。

4 saying "Please look after this bear" の saying は a note を修飾する現在分詞形容詞用法。

5 who meet his disapproval は形容詞節で、関係代名詞の働きは主語。

6 with whom he shares their "elevenses" of buns and cocoa は形容詞節で、関係代名詞の働きは前置詞の目的語。

7 caused by an innocent misunderstanding の caused は trouble を修飾する過去分詞形容詞用法。

　すべてに正解された人は、文章を正確に読む力がかなりついたのだと考えていただいていいかと思います。間違えた人は、準動詞や関係代名詞をきちんと理解できるよう復習しましょう。

Vocabulary Check Before Reading

本文に出てくる単語の意味として正しいものを選択肢の中から選びなさい。

1. stowaway　　**2.** stranger　　**3.** jar　　**4.** disapproval　　**5.** title

ⓐ 表題　　ⓑ ビン　　ⓒ 密航者　　ⓓ 他所から来た熊　　ⓔ 反感

Reading Passage

1 Michael Bond found a lone teddy bear in a London shop near Paddington Station. The bear inspired him to write a book and in 1958 *A Bear Called Paddington* was published.

2 Sent to England as a stowaway from "Darkest Peru" by his Aunt Lucy, the bear arrived at Paddington Station. The Brown family 5 found him sitting on his suitcase, wearing an old bush hat and with a note attached to his coat saying "Please look after this bear." The Brown family fell in love with this new stranger and so named him "Paddington" after the station.

3 Paddington usually wears a blue duffel coat and occasionally a pair 10 of "Wellington Boots." He always carries his battered suitcase and in it is a jar of marmalade because as he says, "bears love marmalade."

4 Paddington is an anthropomorphized bear and he is always kind to others. However he gives "hard stares" to those who meet his disapproval. 15

5 His most favorite friend is Mr. Gruber with whom he shares their "elevenses" of buns and cocoa.

6 Paddington usually meets some trouble caused by an innocent misunderstanding but because of his kind nature, the story usually has a happy or funny ending. 20

7 Paddington Bear consists of 14 collections of different titles with the final one, a picture book. The series has also been adapted for TV and a movie has been made about Paddington Bear.

NOTES

Michael Bond (1926-2017)　イギリスの児童文学者で『くまのパディントン』シリーズの作者
teddy bear　縫いぐるみのクマの人形
Paddington Station　パディントン駅（ロンドンの主要駅の１つ）
A Bear Called Paddington　日本では『くまのパディントン』と訳されている
"Darkest Peru"　「暗黒のペルー」
bush hat　ブッシュハット（つば広の帽子で、オーストラリア軍の制帽）
look after~　〜の世話をする、面倒を見る
fall in love with~　〜に恋する、〜をとても気にいる
name A after B　ＢにちなんでＡと名づける
duffel coat　ダッフルコート（フード付きのコート）
Wellington Boots　ウェリントンブーツ（ひざやふくらはぎまでのゴム製の長靴）
battered　使い古しの
anthropomorphized　擬人化された
hard stare　にらみつける
elevenses　軽食、お茶
buns　ロールパン

(=) Synonyms Check After Reading

本文に出てきた動詞・語句の意味として近いものを選択肢の中から選びなさい。

1. inspire
2. publish
3. send
4. arrive
5. wear
6. carry
7. anthropomorphize
8. cause
9. consist of
10. adapt

ⓐ get to
ⓑ be composed
ⓒ modify
ⓓ dispatch
ⓔ be dressed in
ⓕ personify
ⓖ stimulate
ⓗ issue
ⓘ bring about
ⓙ convey

○× True or False

本文の内容を正しく示している英文には T、誤っている英文には F を記入しなさい。

_____ 1. The bear was sent from darkest Africa by his Aunt Lucy.

_____ 2. The "elevenses" are a lunch break.

_____ 3. Paddington is kind to others and his favorite friend is Mr. Gruber.

Comprehension Check

質問の答えとして正しいものを 3 つの選択肢の中から選びなさい。

1. From what country was the bear sent to England?

    a. Africa   **b.** America   **c.** Peru

2. Who is Paddington's most favorite friend ?

    a. Mr. Gruber   **b.** The Brown family **c.** Aunt Lucy

3. What kind of ending does the story have?

    a. Sad   **b.** Happy   **c.** Tragic

⟩⟩ **Audio 19**

 Listening for Information

音声を聞いて、答えとして正しいものを選択肢の中から選びましょう。本文に出てくる数字などのデータを正しく把握できているか確認しましょう。

1. a. Please look for this bear
   b. Please look at this bear
   c. Please look after this bear

2. a. Marmalade and bread
   b. Marmalade and cocoa
   c. Buns and cocoa

3. a. 11   **b.** 13   **c.** 14

Grammar Tip Before Reading

▶ 副詞節の働き

　この Unit の英文中、どれが副詞節がわかりますか？　この文のどこからどこまでが副詞節か考えてみて下さい。

King forgot his guitar and went back into to get it ⓘ even though it was dangerous.

　①の部分が副詞節です。副詞には４つの働きがあります。❶動詞修飾❷形容詞修飾❸他の副詞修飾❹文修飾の４つです。副詞節の場合は、ほとんどが動詞修飾で、形容詞修飾や他の副詞修飾で使われることは滅多になく、文修飾で使われることはありません。この文の意味は「キングはギターを忘れたので、危険だったけれどギターを取りにいくために (バー) に戻っていった」となります。「危険だったけれど」という副詞節の部分は「(バー) に戻っていった」という動詞の部分を修飾する働きをしています。

　副詞節を作る品詞の代表は従属接続詞です。接続詞には等位接続詞と従属接続詞の２種類あります。 等位接続詞 は文法上対等の関係にある語と語、句と句、節と節を結びつける語で、and, but , or, for, so などがあります。 従属接続詞 は従属接続詞を主節に接続する働きをしている接続詞で、and, but , or, for, so 以外の接続詞はすべて従属接続詞だと考えていいと思います。だだし if, that, whether の３つの従属接続詞は名詞節を作る場合があるので注意が必要です。

　復習になりますが、この Unit の英文で使われている形容詞節とその節中での関係代名詞の働きを考えてみて下さい。１つめは、who brought the blues to America(l. 3)、２つめは、who followed him(l. 12)、ともに関係代名詞の節中での働きは主語です。

Vocabulary Check Before Reading

本文に出てくる単語の意味として正しいものを選択肢の中から選びなさい。

1. plantation　　**2.** gin　　**3.** minister　　**4.** dime　　**5.** kerosene stove

> ⓐ 10 セント硬貨　　ⓑ 綿繰り機　　ⓒ 大農園　　ⓓ 灯油ストーブ　　ⓔ 牧師

Reading Passage

1 What are the Blues? Blues are a feeling — feeling down, alone, needing a job, a woman, a lonely sound, hard times. Blues is Life.

2 A musician who brought the blues to America is B.B. King. Born on a plantation, he worked at a cotton gin as a young man. Given his first guitar by a minister, he was a self taught musician and he earned 5 money working for dimes and at one night stands. Then working as a disc jockey/singer, he was given the nickname "Beale Street Blues Boy" and he played at a radio show "King's Spot." Later his name was shortened to B.B. King. King's style was based on fluid string bending

and a shimmering vibrato. His every-note- 10 counts has been a model for guitarists who followed him. He toured constantly and played at clubs, concert halls, hotels, and universities. His guitar style was instantly recognizable everywhere. 15

3 There is a well known story about his guitar named "Lucille." Two men were fighting in a bar over a woman and overturned a kerosene stove. This caused a fire and everyone escaped the fire. King 20 forgot his guitar and went back in to get it even though it was dangerous. Later he named his guitars Lucille so as to remind him to never argue over a woman!

4 King died in May 2015.

NOTES

Blues 19世紀末ごろにアメリカ南部のアフリカ系アメリカ人によって作り出された音楽。Bluesという名前は、不幸や憂鬱な気分（英語でblueと表現する）をうたった歌に由来する。
hard times つらい時期
B. B. King (1925-2015) アメリカのブルースギタリスト、歌手、作曲家。ブルースの王様と呼ばれている。
self taught 独習の、独学の
one night stands 一夜興行
Beale Street アメリカのテネシー州のメンフィスの繁華街にある音楽のあふれる通り
string ギターの弦
bending 弦を弾いた後で、弦を押さえている指で弦を引っ張って音の高さを変えるギターの演奏法
vibrato 声楽や弦楽器などで声や音を震わせること
every-note-count すべての音符をbendingやvibratoで演奏するキング独特の演奏法
recognizable 見てそれと分かる
Lucille B. B. King愛用のギターの名前。由来は火事を起こした2人の男が争っていた女性の名前が「ルシール」だったことによる。
so as to ~ ~するために
argue over ~ ~のことで口論する

本文に出てきた動詞・語句の意味として近いものを選択肢の中から選びなさい。

1. feel
2. earn
3. shorten
4. shimmer
5. follow
6. tour
7. fight
8. overturn
9. forget
10. argue

ⓐ leave
ⓑ come behind
ⓒ travel around
ⓓ battle
ⓔ quarrel
ⓕ overthrow
ⓖ sense
ⓗ gain
ⓘ abridge
ⓙ shine

○× True or False

本文の内容を正しく示している英文には T、誤っている英文には F を記入しなさい。

_____ 1. B. B. King was born on a plantation and worked at a cotton gin.

_____ 2. He got his first guitar at a music shop.

_____ 3. B. B. King named all of his guitars "Lucy."

Comprehension Check

質問の答えとして正しいものを 3 つの選択肢の中から選びなさい。

1. What kind of music did B. B. King bring to America?

   a. Jazz   **b.** Folk   **c.** Blues

2. What was the name of a radio show where B. B. King played?

   a. King's Spot   **b.** King's Shop   **c.** King's Store

3. Even though the bar was dangerous why did King go back into it?

   a. Because he wanted to get his guitar
   b. Because he wanted to see a woman
   c. Because he wanted to fight two men

Audio 21

Listening for Information

音声を聞いて、答えとして正しいものを選択肢の中から選びましょう。本文に出てくる数字などのデータを正しく把握できているか確認しましょう。

1. a. Working as a guitarist
   b. Working as a singer
   c. Working as a pianist

2. a. Happiness   **b.** Sensation   **c.** Loneliness

3. a. A Stove   **b.** Fighting   **c.** A woman

Grammar

▶ There+is (are)+S の構文

　文頭の There は誘導副詞と呼ばれている副詞です。誘導副詞の there は名詞を修飾できないので、一番相性のいい動詞を名詞の前に引き出しています。

　there には新しい情報を導く働きがあります。

　There is a pen on the desk.　は正しい文ですが、

　There is the pen on the desk. は誤文です。

the という冠詞は that から生じたものですが、こちらも 1 語ですが短縮化されています。a の基本的な意味は、多くのものの中の不特定の 1 つという意味です。それに対して the は特定の 1 つと言う意味で、沢山あるものの中の特定のものを指して使います。従って新情報を導く there+is(are)+S では、すでに出てきている旧情報である the+名詞を主語とする構文は使えませんから、There is the pen on the desk. という文は、The pen is on the desk が正しい文です。

　II. 13-14 の Here are some interesting facts . . .

の Here も there と同じく誘導副詞です。誘導副詞 there, here には聞き手の注意を喚起する働きもしています。文頭の there, here は、これから新しい情報を提示するので耳を傾けるよう合図する働きをしています。例えば、友達にバスが来たことに注意を換気する場合には、Here comes the bus! と文頭に注意を換気する here を付けて表現します。

Vocabulary Check Before Reading

本文に出てくる単語の意味として正しいものを選択肢の中から選びなさい。

1. empire　　**2.** rate　　**3.** landmark　　**4.** airship　　**5.** obsevatory

ⓐ 展望台　　ⓑ 割合　　ⓒ 目印となるもの　　ⓓ 帝国　　ⓔ 飛行船

Reading Passage

1 OMG who's that gorilla climbing the Empire State Building? Built in 1931 at a rate of four and a half floors per week, the Empire State Building became an iconic landmark of New York City. The movie

"King Kong" released in 1933 was a popular movie featuring a famous gorilla and a 5 beautiful woman!

2 "Skyscraper" is a word for tall buildings. Can you guess the meaning why? And in the USA there are many skyscrapers but the Empire State Building is the most easily 10 recognizable one. Approximately 4,000,000 tourists visit the building per year.

3 Here are some interesting facts about the building:

1. There were cafes and stands and water taps on five of the floors so 15 workers would not waste time going to ground level to get lunch or water bottles.

2. The Empire State Building's spire was originally intended to be an airship docking station.

3. It was the world's tallest building for 40 years until the World 20 Trade Center was completed in late 1970.

4. The building has its own Zip code, 10118.

5. The building has been featured in more than 250 movies and also a remake of the original King Kong movie.

6. From street level to the top there are 1,872 steps and there is an 25 annual race up to the 86th floor.

7. On a clear day you can see five states from the observatory.

NOTES

OMG EメールやSNSの投稿などで使用される、Oh my God! や Oh my gosh! の略語。文頭か文末で使用し、感動、喜び等の強い感情を示す。
Empire State Building 1931年に完成して以来、長らく世界一の高層ビルとして知られていた。建設時は地上102階、381メートルの高さであったが、51年に電波塔が増設された結果、現在の高さは約449メートル。

at a rate of ~ ~のペースで	**per ~** ~につき
iconic 代表的な	**skyscraper** 超高層ビル
approximately おおよそ	**water tap** 水道の蛇口
ground level 1階	**water bottle** 飲料水のボトル
spire 塔屋（建物の屋上に突き出した部分）	**docking station** 係留塔
World Trade Center 世界貿易センタービル（New York市のManhattanにあった複合施設。2001年9月11日の同時多発テロで破壊された。）	**zip code** 郵便番号
remake 映画の改作版	**street level** 1階

本文に出てきた動詞・語句の意味として近いものを選択肢の中から選びなさい。

1.	climb	ⓐ	call on
2.	build	ⓑ	lose
3.	become	ⓒ	go up
4.	release	ⓓ	finish
5.	feature	ⓔ	go public
6.	guess	ⓕ	develop into
7.	visit	ⓖ	estimate
8.	waste	ⓗ	characterize
9.	intend	ⓘ	plan
10.	complete	ⓙ	construct

⭕❌ True or False

本文の内容を正しく示している英文には T、誤っている英文には F を記入しなさい。

_____ **1.** A famous gorilla named King Kong climbed the World Trade Center.

_____ **2.** There is a race held every five years up to the 86th floor.

_____ **3.** On a clear day you can see New York, New Jersey, Pennsylvania, Connecticut and Massachusetts.

Comprehension Check

質問の答えとして正しいものを3つの選択肢の中から選びなさい。

1. What does the word "skyscraper" mean?

    a. A big building   **b.** An old building   **c.** A tall building

2. Until when was the Empire State Building the world' tallest one?

    a. In late 1970   **b.** In 1933   **c.** In 1872

3. How many steps are there from the street level to the top of the Empire State Building?

    a. 1,782   **b.** 1,872   **c.** 1,827

 Audio 23

Listening for Information

音声を聞いて、答えとして正しいものを選択肢の中から選びましょう。本文に出てくる数字などのデータを正しく把握できているか確認しましょう。

1. a. In 1931   **b.** In 1933   **c.** In 1970

2. a. About 40,000   **b.** About 400,000   **c.** About 4,000,000

3. a. 10118   **b.** 10181   **c.** 10818

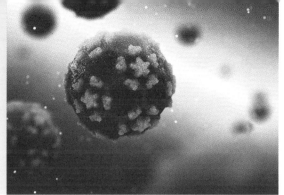

UNIT

12 Dr. Jonas E. Salk

Grammar Tip Before Reading

▶ 名詞節と強調構文

　この Unit で使用されている名詞節について説明します。

The 1950s — Every summer Americans <u>feared</u> that the polio virus would rear its ugly head and infect people all over the USA.

　that から最後の the USA までが名詞節で、動詞 feared の目的語（節）の働きをしています。英語で名詞節を作る語は、❶疑問詞❷従属接続詞の that, if, whether ❸関係代名詞の what ❹関係詞＋ ever（複合関係詞と呼ばれています）❺先行詞の省略された関係副詞の5つです。❹❺は使用頻度が高くはありませんが、❶❷❸は使用頻度が高いので覚えておきましょう。

　この Unit の英文中で強調構文が3つ使われています。

It was Dr. Salk, a medical researcher and virologist, who was first to successfully replicate a safe polio virus.

it was Salk who used the "killed" and safer virus to produce the polio vaccine that bore his name.

although it was Sabin's method that was eventually used worldwide です。

最初と2つ目の例では、it was—who の—の部分が強調されており、3つ目の例では、it was—that の—の部分が強調されています。it was—who も it was—that も意味的な働きはしておらず、強調部分を目立たせるための枠組みとして機能しています。従って上記の文で it was 及び who または that を取り除いても完全な文になります。この強調構文にはもう1つの捉え方があります。それは who と that を関係代名詞と考え、it を先行詞として解釈する捉え方です。この解釈法に従うと、it was—who も it was—that も—の箇所が強調された訳し方になり、誤訳することはないでしょう。

Vocabulary Check Before Reading

本文に出てくる単語の意味として正しいものを選択肢の中から選びなさい。

1. disease　　**2.** capability　　**3.** muscle　　**4.** method　　**5.** medicine

ⓐ 薬　　ⓑ 病気　　ⓒ 筋肉　　ⓓ 方法　　ⓔ 能力

🔊 **Audio 24**

Reading Passage

1 The 1950s – Every summer Americans feared that the polio virus would rear its ugly head and infect people all over the USA. Young children in particular were vulnerable to this disease which attacked the human muscular system. There were photos of young children lying in a huge "iron lung" because children could not breathe on their ⁵ own, having lost all capability to use their muscles to breathe.

2 Two physicians were racing against time to come up with a vaccine to combat this feared disease, Dr. Jonas E. Salk and Dr. Albert Sabin. It was Dr. Salk, a medical researcher and virologist, who was first to successfully replicate a safe polio virus. At that time live strains ¹⁰ of the polio virus were used but it was Salk who used the "killed" and safer virus to produce the polio vaccine that bore his name. After field testing both on animals and children, his virus ¹⁵ was declared safe and immediately a nationwide vaccination program was put into place in 1955. Children of elementary school age were vaccinated nationwide, something which I ²⁰ remember to this day. The vaccine produced antibodies which then protected the body from contracting the disease.

Structure of Polio

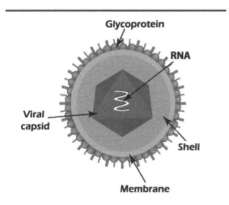

3 Salk was declared a hero and although it was Sabin's method that was eventually used worldwide, Salk's vaccine was declared to be one ²⁵ of the "Essential Medicines" by WHO.

NOTES

polio virus　ポリオウイルス（小児麻痺の原因となるウイルス）
rear its ugly head　悪いことが出現する
in particular　特に
be vulnerable to~　（病気に）かかりやすい
iron lung　鉄の肺（小児麻痺患者などに使う鉄製呼吸補助装置）
on one's own　独力で
physician　内科医　　　　　　　　　　race against time　急いで行なう
Dr. Jonas E. Salk（1914–95）　ポリオワクチンを開発したアメリカの医学者
Dr. Albert Sabin（1906–93）　経口ポリオワクチンを開発したアメリカの医学者
virologist　ウイルス学者
live strain　生きた細胞菌
to this day　今日まで
antibody　抗体
WHO　World Health Organization（世界保健機関）の略語。保健衛生の分野で国際協力をおこなうために設立された国連の専門機関の一つ。

本文に出てきた動詞・語句の意味として近いものを選択肢の中から選びなさい。

1. fear   ⓐ be afraid of

2. rear   ⓑ transmit

3. infect   ⓒ act against

4. attack   ⓓ catch

5. lie   ⓔ copy

6. race   ⓕ find out

7. come up with ⓖ compete

8. replicate   ⓗ show to be

9. declare   ⓘ rest

10. contract   ⓙ raise

○× True or False

本文の内容を正しく示している英文には T、誤っている英文には F を記入しなさい。

_____ **1.** While polio virus infected humans of all ages, young children were particularly vulnerable.

_____ **2.** The "killed" type of virus was not very effective against the disease.

_____ **3.** The author was a young boy when he was vaccinated.

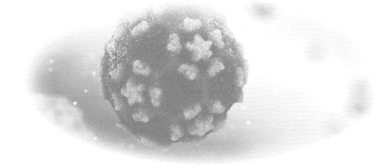

Comprehension Check

質問の答えとして正しいものを 3 つの選択肢の中から選びなさい。

1. Who in particular were vulnerable to polio virus?

   a. Babies   **b.** Children   **c.** Adults

2. Why did young children lie in a huge "iron lung"?

   a. Because they could breathe for themselves.
   b. Because they could not breathe for themselves.
   c. Because they could breathe on their own.

3. After Salk's virus was declared safe, where was Sabin's method used?

   a. All over the world   **b.** In the UK   **c.** In the USA

🔊 Audio 25

 ## Listening for Information

音声を聞いて、答えとして正しいものを選択肢の中から選びましょう。本文に出てくる数字などのデータを正しく把握できているか確認しましょう。

1. a. In the 1940s   **b.** In the 1950s   **c.** In the1960s

2. a. Two   **b.** Three   **c.** Four

3. a. Animal testing
   b. Children testing
   c. Animal and children testing

13 Trick or Treat!!

Grammar Tip Before Reading

▶ 準動詞と従属節の復習（1）

準動詞の種類（⇒ Unit 9）と働き、従属節の場合は種類（名詞節、形容詞節、副詞節）と節の始まりと終わり、その働きを答えてみましょう。

準動詞（冒頭は段落番号）：

imported from the U. S. A は festival を修飾する過去分形容詞用法　influenced by Christianity は pagan roots を修飾する過去分形容詞用法　2 known as "All Hallows Eve" は November 1st and 2nd を修飾する過去分形容詞用法　3 to be eaten は不定詞名詞または形容詞用法で動詞 made の目的格補語　4 offering は分詞構文で動詞 went を修飾している　4 to pray は不定詞で動詞 offer の目的語　4 returning は those を修飾する現在分形容詞用法　4 Believing は分詞構文で動詞 said を修飾している　4 meaning は "trick or treat" を修飾する現在分形容詞用法　5 lighted は candle を修飾する過去分形容詞用法　5 to ward off は不定詞で動詞 was placed を修飾する副詞修飾　6 dressed up は分詞構文で、動詞 go を修飾している。

名詞節と副詞節：

1 where Halloween originate は名詞節で前置詞 about の目的語　3 that the souls... during their return は名詞節で動詞 believed の目的語　4 that the costumes... them alone は名詞節で動詞 believing の目的語　4 if they did not receive a treat (soul cake) は副詞節で動詞 play を修飾している。　4 "trick or treat"... (soul cake) は名詞節で動詞 said の目的語（ここでは、"trick or treat" の前に接続詞の that が省略されている）。

Vocabulary Check Before Reading

本文に出てくる単語の意味として正しいものを選択肢の中から選びなさい。

1. festival　　**2.** roots　　**3.** soul　　**4.** ghost　　**5.** exchange

ⓐ お祭り　　ⓑ 魂　　ⓒ 交換　　ⓓ 幽霊　　ⓔ 出自

Reading Passage

1 Have you ever thought about where Halloween originated? In Japan it is simply a festival imported from the USA. However it has Celtic pagan roots later influenced by Christianity.

2 Halloween occurred on the eve of October 31st and before the holy days of November 1st and 2nd, collectively known as "All Hallows Eve." Therefore the name became "Halloween" but many centuries later it gradually lost its original meaning.

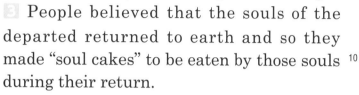

3 People believed that the souls of the departed returned to earth and so they made "soul cakes" to be eaten by those souls during their return.

4 Poor children then dressed up in simple "ghost" or "devil" costumes and went around town offering to pray for those returning souls in exchange for soul cakes. Believing that the costumes would protect them from real evil spirits and leave them alone, children often said "trick or treat" meaning they would play a trick on the homeowner if they did not receive a treat (soul cake).

5 A pumpkin jack-o'-lantern was often placed in a window and a candle lighted inside to ward off any possible evil spirits from entering that home.

6 So nowadays dressed up in various costumes, children go trick or treating in their neighborhoods. Adults have parties and there are contests for the best or most unusual costume.

7 Vampires and ghosts and Darth Vader!!! You better be careful!

NOTES

Halloween　諸聖人の祝日の前夜（10月31日）のお祭り。秋の収穫を祝い悪霊を追い出す古代ケルト人の祭りが起源。

Celtic　ケルト族の（インドーヨーロッパ語系のヨーロッパ先住民）

pagan　異教徒の　　　　　　　　Christianity　キリスト教

the departed　亡くなった人々　　　soul cake　円形または楕円形の甘い菓子パン

in exchange for~　～と交換に

trick or treat　「お菓子をちょうだい、くれないといたずらするよ」Halloween の晩に近所を回った時に、お菓子やお金をねだる時に発する言葉。

homeowner　家主　　　　　　　　pumpkin　カボチャ

Jack 'o Lantern　カボチャ（など）のちょうちん（中身をくりぬき、目、口、鼻などをあけたもの。おもに Halloween に子供が作って遊ぶ。

ward off　追い払う

Vampire　吸血鬼（死体から蘇り寝ている人の血を吸うといわれる悪霊）

Darth Vader　ダース・ベイダー（映画 Star Wars シリーズに登場する悪役の武将）

(=) Synonyms

本文に出てきた動詞・語句の意味として近いものを選択肢の中から選びなさい。

1. originate
2. import
3. influence
4. occur
5. return
6. offer
7. pray
8. protect
9. place
10. light

ⓐ illuminate
ⓑ put
ⓒ guard
ⓓ worship
ⓔ propose
ⓕ come back
ⓖ happen
ⓗ affect
ⓘ introduce
ⓙ begin

○× True or False

本文の内容を正しく示している英文には T、誤っている英文には F を記入しなさい。

_____ **1.** Halloween was strictly a Christian holiday.

_____ **2.** Halloween is similar to the Obon Festival held in August.

_____ **3.** Nowadays people have parties and children go trick or treating.

Comprehension Check

質問の答えとして正しいものを 3 つの選択肢の中から選びなさい。

1. When did Halloween occur?

   a. Before the eve of October 31st
   b. On the eve of October 31st
   c. After the eve of October 31st

2. Whose souls were believed to eat "soul cakes"?

   a. Children   **b.** Grown-ups   **c.** The dead

3. Why was a pumpkin jack o' lantern often placed in a window?

   a. To drive away evil spirits.
   b. To drive away evil children.
   c. To welcome children.

.))) Audio 27

 Listening for Information

音声を聞いて、答えとして正しいものを選択肢の中から選びましょう。本文に出てくる数字などのデータを正しく把握できているか確認しましょう。

1. a. Germany   **b.** The UK   **c.** The USA

2. a. Sea   **b.** Earth   **c.** Heaven

3. a. In a Kitchen   **b.** At a door   **c.** In a window

Do You Know These Idioms?

Grammar Tip Before Reading

▶ 準動詞と従属節の復習（2）

この Unit の英文中から準動詞と節を見つけ出し、その種類と働きを考えてみましょう。

なお、**1**などの囲み数字は p. 57 の Reading Passage の段落番号を示しています。

準動詞

2 playing field の playing は動名詞。ここでは playing field を 1 つの名詞として扱う。

2 to be successful と to have の前に be going to が使われていることに注意。

2 have to も助動詞として扱うので、to hit も不定詞として扱わない

2 to pinch hit は不定詞の名詞用法で動詞 bring の目的語

2 to meet up with は不定詞の名詞用法で動詞 ask の目的語

2 to "bring home the bacon" は不定詞の名詞用法で動詞 help の目的語

4 to keep negotiating は不定詞の名詞用法で動詞 is の補語。negotiating は動名詞で動詞 keep の目的語。

形容詞節・名詞節・副詞節

1 which give extra meaning and color to the language は形容詞節で名詞 idioms を修飾

1 what this dialog means は名詞節で動詞 guess の目的語

2 they are having with another company は形容詞節で名詞 negotiations を修飾

2 we were "in the home stretch" は名詞節で動詞 thought の目的語

2 what I really dislike は名詞節で主語

2 when we're not on an "even playing field" は名詞節で動詞 is の補語。この when は ごく稀に従属接続詞が名詞節を作る例。

2 if we're going to be successful は副詞節で動詞 hit を修飾

2 he can help to "bring home the bacon" は名詞節で形容詞 sure の目的語。he の前に 従属接続詞 that が省略されている。

Vocabulary Check Before Reading

本文に出てくる単語の意味として正しいものを選択肢の中から選びなさい。

1. dialogue　**2.** negotiation　**3.** company　**4.** exception　**5.** interference

ⓐ 交渉　　ⓑ 対話　　ⓒ 会社　　ⓓ 妨害、干渉　　ⓔ 例外

Reading Passage

1 All languages have idioms which give extra meaning and color to the language. English is the same. Can you guess what this dialog means?

2 John and Rick are discussing the negotiations they are having with another company.

5

John: I thought we were "in the homestretch" but they "moved the goal posts" on us.

Rick: Yeah, what I really dislike is when we're not on an "even playing field."

John: Well, if we're going to be successful, 10 we're going to have to "hit the ball out of the park." We really need a "four bagger" this time around.

Rick: You know, Mike usually has the "inside track" with this company. Maybe we should bring him up "to pinch hit" for us. We should go for a "full court press." 15

John: Good idea! I'll "get on the horn" and ask him to meet up with us tomorrow. I'm sure he can help to "bring home the bacon."

3 With the exception of two idioms all of the others are sports idioms. Can you guess which sports?

4 Here's another short dialog. Good luck! 20

John: OK, our "game plan" is to keep negotiating until the "clock runs out."

Rick: Right, Mike will be "running interference" for us on this one. He's the "point man."

John: Great, but we may have "to punt" and do "an end run" around 25 them.

NOTES

in the homestretch　仕事の最終部分、追い込み、山場
move the goal posts　都合がいいように条件・規則を変更する
playing field　平等な立場　　　　　　　hit the ball out of the park　予想以上の成果を挙げる
four bagger　ホームラン　　　　　　　　this time around　今度こそ、ここは一つ
inside track　友好な関係　　　　　　　　to pinch hit　代役を務める
full court press　全力投球をする　　　　get on the horn　電話をかける
bring home the bacon　期待通りの成果を挙げる
with the exception of ~　~を除いて、例外として
Good luck　頑張ってね　　　　　　　　game plan　作戦
until "the clock runs out"　ぎりぎりの時間まで　running interference　厄介な問題を前もって処理する
point man　先頭に立ち活躍する人　　　to punt　別の手を使う
an end run　うまくかわす

本文に出てきた動詞・語句の意味として近いものを選択肢の中から選びなさい。

1. give   ⓐ strike

2. color   ⓑ request

3. discuss   ⓒ hold talks

4. dislike   ⓓ tint

5. hit   ⓔ propose

6. ask   ⓕ rendezvous

7. meet up with ⓖ save

8. bring   ⓗ present with

9. keep   ⓘ talk over

10. negotiate   ⓙ hate

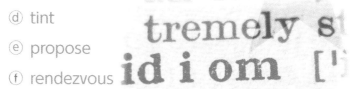

○× **True or False**

本文の内容を正しく示している英文には T、誤っている英文には F を記入しなさい。

_____ **1.** "Inside track" is catching a train inside a station.

_____ **2.** "Bring home the bacon" means to go to the supermarket to buy some bacon.

_____ **3.** Mike is an important man for the negotiations.

Comprehension Check

質問の答えとして正しいものを 3 つの選択肢の中から選びなさい。

1. How many languages have idioms?

　a. Some languages
　b. Many languages
　c. All languages

2. What does "hit the ball out of the park?

　a. Do a great job
　b. Hit a single
　c. Hit a home run

3. What sport is the idiom, "four bagger" related to?

　a. soccer　　**b.** baseball　　**c.** basketball

.)) Audio 29

 Listening for Information

音声を聞いて、答えとして正しいものを選択肢の中から選びましょう。本文に出てくる数字などのデータを正しく把握できているか確認しましょう。

1. a. Strange meaning
　b. Extra meaning
　c. Surprising meaning

2. a. Basketball　　　**b.** Baseball　　　**c.** Soccer

3. a. Send an email
　b. Make a telephone call
　c. Write a business letter

15 Windsor Castle

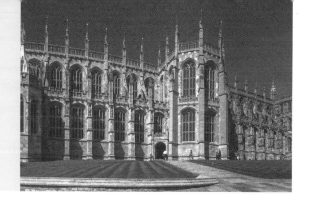

Grammar Tip Before Reading

▶準動詞と従属節の復習（3）

　この Unit の英文中から準動詞と節を見つけ出し、その種類と働きを考えてみましょう。

準動詞：

1 Build（l. 1）は分詞構文で動詞 is を修飾

1 extending（l. 1）は分詞構文で動詞 is を修飾

1 occupied（l. 3）は過去分詞形容詞で castle を修飾

1 to protect（l. 3）は不定詞副詞用法で動詞 was built を修飾

1 visiting（l. 7）は現在分形容詞で名詞 heads of states を修飾

2 Needless to say（l. 8）は熟語なので不定詞には含まない。

2 based（l. 10）は過去分詞形容詞用法で名詞 Georgian and Victorian design を修飾

3 forming（l. 13）は現在分詞形容詞用法で名詞 The State Apartments を修飾

3 Dating（l. 16）は現在分詞形容詞用法で名詞 St. George's Chapel を修飾

4 designed（l. 16）は過去分詞形容詞用法で名詞 St. George's Chapel を修飾

4 including（l. 18）は現在分詞形容詞用法で名詞 parkland を修飾

形容詞節：

1 which she uses on weekends（l. 6）は形容詞節で名詞 the official residence of the Queen（ll. 5-6）を修飾

Vocabulary Check Before Reading

本文に出てくる単語の意味として正しいものを選択肢の中から選びなさい。

1. dominance　　**2.** battle　　**3.** residence　　**4.** banquet　　**5.** in essence

ⓐ 戦い　　ⓑ 晩餐会　　ⓒ 支配　　ⓓ 邸宅、官邸　　ⓔ 本質的には

.))) **Audio 30**

Reading Passage

1 Built in the 11th century since the time of Henry I and extending to the 21st century and Queen Elizabeth, Windsor Castle is the longest occupied castle in Europe! It was originally built to protect the Norman dominance around the River Thames and has endured wars and battles over the centuries. It is now the official residence of the ₅ Queen which she uses on weekends. It is also the site for official state banquets for heads of state visiting the U.K.

2 Needless to say it is a popular tourist attraction and the castle combines the features of a fortification, a castle and a small town. It is in essence a Georgian and Victorian design based on a Medieval ₁₀ structure with Gothic features.

3 The Castle consists of the Middle Ward, Upper Ward and Lower Ward. The State Apartments forming the major part of the Upper Ward were designed by Wyatville in the 19th century. Different rooms follow Classic, Gothic and Rococo styles. ₁₅

4 Dating from late 15th century and designed in Perpendicular Gothic style is St. George's Chapel next to the Lower Ward. The castle is surrounded by a parkland including two working farms and estate cottages.

5 Windsor Castle survived a rather devastating fire in 1992 but it ₂₀ has since been restored.

6 A popular feature is the daily Changing of the Guard at 11:00 a.m. This is free.

NOTES

　　Windsor Castle　ロンドン西郊のウインザーにあるイギリス王室の離宮　**Henry I**（1068–1135）ヘンリー1世（ノルマン朝のイングランド王で、征服王ウイリアム1世の末子）　**Queen Elizabeth**（1926– ）エリザベス1世、英国女王（ジョージ6世の子で1952年に即位）　**occupied**　人が住んでいる　　**Norman dominance**　ノルマン人の支配（1066年にノルマンディー公ウイリアムズがイングランドに侵入し、イギリスを支配した）　**River Thames**　ロンドンを貫流して北海に注ぐイングランド南部の河　　**heads of states**　国家元首　**U. K**　United Kingdom(of Great Britain and Northern Ireland)「グレート・ブリテンおよび北アイルランド連合王国」イギリスの正式な国名の省略形　**needless to say**　言うまでもなく　**fortification**　要塞　**Georgian**　イギリスの George 王朝（1714–1830）時代の　**Victorian**　イギリスの Victoria 女王（1819–1901）時代の　**Gothic**　12–16世紀に中世西ヨーロッパで用いられた建築、絵画、彫刻などの様式　**Middle Ward, Upper Ward, Lower Ward**　ウィンザー城はミドル・ウォード（中郭）、アッパー・ウォード（上郭）、ロワー・ウォード（下郭）に分かれている。　**the State Apartments**　儀式用の広間　**Classic**　古典的な　**Rococo**　ロココ様式（18世紀に流行した曲線を使った繊細さ、優美さが特徴の様式）　**Perpendicular Gothic style**　14–15世紀の英国の末期ゴシック様式で垂直線を強調するところに特徴がある　**St. George Chapel**　Windsor 城内にある15世紀のゴシック建築　**working farm**　農園　**estate cottage**　所有の別荘　**devastating fire in 1992**　1992年に北東部のチェスター・タワーにある礼拝堂から出火した大火事　**daily Changing of the Guard**　4月–7月は日曜を除く毎日、それ以外の月は月曜、水曜、金曜、土曜の11:00–11:45の45分間衛兵の交代式が見学できる。

(≡) Synonyms Check After Reading

本文に出てきた動詞・語句の意味として近いものを選択肢の中から選びなさい。

1. extend
2. endure
3. form
4. design
5. follow
6. date
7. surround
8. include
9. survive
10. restore

ⓐ repair
ⓑ start
ⓒ contain
ⓓ imitate
ⓔ shape
ⓕ undergo
ⓖ encircle
ⓗ lay out
ⓘ stay behind
ⓙ continue

○× True or False

本文の内容を正しく示している英文には T、誤っている英文には F を記入しなさい。

_____ 1. Windsor Castle has a long history dating back to Henry I.

_____ 2. Queen Elizabeth resides there on a daily basis.

_____ 3. The castle is surrounded by a large suburban town.

Comprehension Check

質問の答えとして正しいものを3つの選択肢の中から選びなさい。

1. Who lives now in Windsor Castle on weekends?

   a. Henry I   **b.** Queen Elizabeth   **c.** Wyatville

2. How many Wards is Windsor Castle consisted of?

   a. Two   **b.** Three   **c.** Four

3. What happened in 1992?

   a. A big fire
   b. Restoration of Windsor Castle
   c. Daily Changing of the Guard

Audio 31

 ## Listening for Information

音声を聞いて、答えとして正しいものを選択肢の中から選びましょう。本文に出てくる数字などのデータを正しく把握できているか確認しましょう。

1. a. Henry I
   b. Queen Elizabeth
   c. Wyatville

2. a. The official residence for heads of state visiting the U.K.
   b. The official state banquets for heads of state visiting the U.K.
   c. The parkland including two working farms and estate cottages

3. a. Georgian and Victorian
   b. Gothic
   c. Rococo

Enjoying American & British Culture Using Grammar Tips
文法ヒントで楽しむ英米文化リーディング

2020 年 4 月 10 日　初版第 1 刷発行

著　者　Richard Carpenter ／森永弘司

発行者　森　信久
発行所　**株式会社　松 柏 社**
　　　　〒 102-0072　東京都千代田区飯田橋 1-6-1
　　　　TEL　03 (3230) 4813（代表）
　　　　FAX　03 (3230) 4857
　　　　http://www.shohakusha.com
　　　　e-mail: info@shohakusha.com

装　帧　　　　小島トシノブ（NONdesign）
本文レイアウト　株式会社クリエーターズユニオン（一柳 茂）
印刷・製本　　中央精版印刷株式会社

略号 = 760

ISBN978-4-88198-760-5